I Need A Boost

"What's Driving You Could Be Draining You"

Mansfield Key, III

ISBN: 9798850520342

Go Get It Publishing, LLC
Tuscaloosa, Alabama

Acknowledgements & Dedication

Every good work requires the effort of a team. Therefore, I acknowledge all the people who have supported me throughout the journey of completing this good word. In addition, I feel compelled to make dedications to specific people in my life.

This book is dedicated to all the great writers in my family: my mother, Shirley Key; my grandmother, Geneva Dortch Brown; and my Great Grandfather, Stroke "Pappa" Dortch. They all passed away before they wrote their manuscripts, but their spirit lives through my writing.

To my wife, Sharlene, who has been my friend, my love, and my biggest supporter since middle school. To my daughters, Erin and Joi, for their patience and understanding during the writing process. Thanks to my Dad and my two brothers for believing in me and supporting my dreams.

Special thanks to the D'Undray Peterson, Anthony Brooks, Dede Simmons, Juanica Baugh, Pastor Marcus Motton, Dr. Jimmy Shaw, Dr. Eric Mackey, Pastor James Edwards, Bernard Baugh, Louis Gordon, De'Shaunna Parker, Nancy Gonce, Harry Smith, and Alison M. Caddell.

This book was crafted explicitly for; teachers, counselors, principals, superintendents, professors, support personnel, secretaries, accountants, librarians, information technology personnel, coaches, athletic directors, maintenance staff, social workers, nurses, cafeteria workers, instructional coaches, curriculum coordinators, school psychologists, school therapists, mental health coordinators, and anyone else working in education. "I Need a Boost" is suitable for those experiencing compassion fatigue or burnout and those seeking tools to maintain their passion for what they do. Everyone can relate to being driven by the same thing draining them and needing a boost to sustain energy and passion sometime.

Foreword

Twenty-two years and nine months; that is how long I have been in the field of education. I have been an administrator for sixteen of those years and a superintendent for six. In those 273 months of service, I have never met a human being that can impact students, parents, teachers, administrators, business leaders, or community members like Mansfield (Pete) Key III. If there was ever an individual equipped to talk about giving people from any walk of life a boost, it is Mansfield Key III.

In life, some individuals leave a mark on anyone that they meet. Mansfield "Ole Pete Key" Key III is one such person. Mansfield, or Pete, as he is best known in North Alabama, has left a legacy by walking his talk. His presence has made a difference for generations, races, and genders of people from Alabama to South Africa and everywhere in between. In short, Pete's presence is significant. I humbly write this foreword as a man who is not worthy of holding his sandals when I think about his positive impact on students in families in Florence, Alabama, our hometown. *I Need a Boost* will illuminate what makes Mansfield Key III remarkable; he is a force, blessed by God, to lift the lives of others to higher heights. *I need a boost* will give you a boost.

Pete has been a leader since his early school days. His intellect went beyond what the naked eye could see. What he was able to face and overcome gives him the credibility to give any of us a boost. His insatiable desire to win at life drove him down many paths, and no matter the path, Pete was always leading. As he matured and grew, he learned to take those leadership skills to make the lives of young people and all people better. I have had the privilege of watching him first impact high school girls that did not have the skill set to resolve conflict. What we saw was a master teacher. But it was more than reading and math. We saw a master teach life skills, conflict resolution skills, communication skills, grit, and growth mindset skills, all from a place of achievement from his trials and then triumphs. That is why he can give you a boost. He knows what it is to be low and then rise high. His desire has not been for personal fortune or fame. It has been to turn back and help those around him that need the help. He has chosen to impact Florence, Alabama, with the significance of his presence, but we are not big enough to stop or contain his impact from spreading to the world.

From his groundbreaking contributions to early learning, adult motivation, and student decision-making skills, his tireless efforts in championing the importance of people being present to help people, to his transformative role in relentlessly pursuing the elimination of adult professional burnout, Mansfield Key III is a force of positive nature that the world needs, and more importantly, that you need.

Mansfield Key III is a father. He is a husband. He is a son. He is a brother. He is an uncle. He is a friend. He is a human that has answered his call to serve. He is an everyday man that has overcome extraordinary things to impact the world. He is a man of character that has a commitment to empower others. Behind every drive to be successful lies a man or woman driven by a profound sense of purpose that is often driven by personal setbacks or failure. The same fire that consumes some people will fuel others with an unrelenting drive toward their purpose. Pete Key's purpose is rooted in other people's success and his relentless desire to make the world better through the power of his significant presence and words.

As you dig into the pages of *I Need a Boost*, be prepared to be faced with the deep emotions that come from experiences of triumph, adversity, and dreams that were deferred but not denied. Through the stories held within these pages, you will feel the transformative power of Mansfield Key III's words, presence, and unwavering belief in the power of our beliefs and significant presence to create meaningful change in the lives of others. This book is a testament to the power of passion, perseverance, and the pursuit of excellence. It is a series of living testimonies to all who read it of the capacity that we all possess to make a difference despite whatever challenges we face and to embrace the dark of now because we know that a brighter tomorrow is possible for us all.

As you embark on this life journey inside the pages of this book, get your heart and mind ready to be captivated by Mansfield Key III's life lessons. His story will serve as a light for those in a seemingly inexorable dark. His words will ignite the light within you to dream big, take the road less traveled, and know that we all have a moral obligation to leave a legacy of significance in our lives that will shape the world for generations to come. This book will sharpen your greatest tools, your heart, mind, and emotions.

Whether you are an educator or a Fortune 500 executive, if you are looking for the spark to reignite your purpose, rediscover your passion, and rekindle the power within you, *I Need a Boost* is the right book for you, and Mansfield Key III is the author that can take you there. Sit back and learn what people from Alabama to South Africa and everywhere have learned. Mansfield Pete Key III was put on this earth to boost you. Enjoy.

Dr. Jimmy Shaw

Preface

Thursday, March 12, 2020, in Knoxville, Tennessee, I had just spoken to the Tennessee Volunteers' entire football team and staff. This presentation was one of the most potent sessions on Title IV for a college program ever. Coaches, players, administrators, and the Athletic Director were in awe over the mixture of drama, music, and motivational teaching on such a unique topic. I never imagined that 24 hours later, life would change forever.

It all started the next day when we heard that the NBA wouldn't be playing games because of the COVID-19 outbreak. Flights were canceled. Grocery stores were running out of wipes and tissues rapidly, and the world began to panic. One death after another death – while masks and hand sanitizer suddenly became crucial components of daily life. The world started to look different.

Monday morning came, and I started receiving emails that almost every speaking engagement that I had was canceled indefinitely for the next year. Every contract but one was canceled, and we went from a bright future of speaking engagements to almost zero. In addition, I didn't qualify for PPP loans or unemployment; I had one daughter in college and the other daughter about to be a freshman with no scholarship. Life looked hopeless.

In such unprecedented times, I had no roadmap, no answers from the government (local or federal), and everyone was stuck at home. We had just closed the deal on our dream home, and now we were on the verge of being forced out of it. Four banks and a credit institution denied us because we could not show any current or future income to close on the house, a house we had already signed a purchasing contract to buy. Soon after, one daughter came home from college because of a mandate requiring her to stay, while our youngest daughter was hoping to attend school in the fall with no scholarship or money.

Before this time, cancer had been the big C-word to strike fear in the hearts of many when it came to healthcare. Now there was a new c-word, except this one wasn't an exception impacting some – it impacted the entire world at one time. COVID-19 stay-at-home mandates were an international phenomenon for all except essential workers. The tensions created by the George Floyd incident only pushed the public further to the edge. Health fears were rampant, racial tension was high, the political scene was divisive – and I was secretly experiencing a silent crisis.

I woke up one morning at about 3:00 am, and my heart was beating fast. I was soaking wet with sweat and breathing hard. I got out of bed, left the bedroom, and walked into my office area as I pondered my thoughts and reviewed my options. *Do we move? Do I get a job?* But no one was hiring during the pandemic! *Do I take the offer we received a few months before the pandemic that required us to move 7 hours away?*

What do you do when you're about to lose your dream home before purchasing it? What do you tell your youngest daughter, who believes she is going to college at the school of her choice when you suddenly cannot afford it? What do you tell your oldest daughter in her second year of college as you fear she's unable to return to school? I didn't know the answer to these questions, and I struggled with the confinement created by the stay-at-home mandate. We were all sitting in the house in fear of COVID while trying to cope with life.

I was watching my life crumble while the news showed the world was doing the same. The thing that had once brought me great joy and hope for the future was now causing great despair and fear. What once filled me with laughter and hope now had me crying with anxious thoughts of the future. I started hearing the voice of my dad when, earlier in my life, he once said, "Go get a real job at the plant, son. Speaking is not a real job – it doesn't pay."

Other voices got louder and louder – the voices of haters and critics. *You don't have it. You will always be unsuccessful. You needed help to read in school – what makes you think you can help others?* I pondered back and forth over every possible solution I could think of at the time. *If we relocate, I can start over, get a loan and get the girls into school. If I get another job locally, I can save and show we have income, and we can keep the house.* We had made good money for years but were watching the savings go dwindling to nothing.

My wife and I pondered every scenario we could think of and still couldn't find any answers. A few days later, seemingly out of nowhere, we got an email from a program in Arkansas.

Mr. Key, you may not remember me, but you motivated our staff, and it changed the trajectory of our district. Our program was experiencing high turnover rates, burnout, and compassion fatigue was at an all-time high, and when you came, you changed our mindset. My staff still talks about your keynote address that had us laughing, crying, dancing, and most of all; it gave us the motivation we needed. Your presentation was entitled "I Need a Boost," and our state needs your message now more than ever. Would you contract with us to do a virtual presentation on Zoom? We have teachers, social workers, nurses, and principals within our entire district that need you.

Ironically, they called me to speak to an audience that needed a boost when I needed the same thing for myself. What do you do when people call you to provide them with what they need when it's a need you lack as well? That's when I realized the concept of "what's driving you could be draining you."

This concept – "what's driving you could be draining you" – is not an abstract theoretical change modification process that has 40 years of research that's been studied extensively at the University. It is not a ten-step theory or a philosophy on how to get a boost in life and become a millionaire. Instead, this is a book full of real stories of people who have struggled, strived, and overcome various circumstances to keep them going when they wanted to quit and throw in the towel. This book has several stories of resilient people who have passion and purpose but struggle with low pay and performance sometimes because they lack motivation.

This book is inspired by my struggles in 2020 because the same thing that was driving me was draining me. The same thing they wanted me to give the educators in Arkansas was the same thing I needed for myself. I had done the "I Need a Boost" keynote address for years, but it took on an entirely different meaning when I was experiencing it while sharing it. I didn't know at the time that what was a keynote address then would be the book you're reading now.

Suddenly, from that day forward, I envisioned myself with booster cables around my neck, symbolically connecting to people to help jump-start their day. I signed the contract to do several presentations with the state of Arkansas. The University of Tennessee called me back to do another presentation to the football team. The University of North Alabama (a school that's literally in my back yard) asked me to contract with the Athletic Department to work with all student-athletes, coaches, and admin staff as the Coordinator of Student-Athlete Development.

In the middle of June, my daughter got a letter with a full-ride scholarship to the university she had dreamed about attending since she was a child. Six months later, we finished closing on that dream home. And suddenly, we looked up to find that the pandemic was over, and my wife and I were empty nesters.

The one thing I realized after the pandemic was that people needed hope. People were experiencing burnout and compassion fatigue from all walks of life, looking for hope and a boost. We realized people were being driven and drained by the same thing. The call from Arkansas – the one that essentially said, "My people need a boost, and you're the perfect person to help us pivot and shift" – that call did more for me than it did for them. It showed me a truth about myself and so many others. Everyone who works a job, owns a company, or runs a program can be driven and drained at the same time by the same thing.

The Superintendent, driven by feeding and leading the district to get favorable results, can also get drained in doing so. The social worker who gets the adrenaline rush from helping others can also get fatigued by the same clients. The company owner, driven by helping people and making money, can also get exhausted in assisting and making money. Everyone is driven by something or someone, but we can also be drained by something or someone.

Can you imagine driving down the highway and the low fuel light comes on to show that the vehicle needs gas and there's not a filling station within miles? Can you imagine getting to the station and the gas station is out of gas? You have the car, but you cannot move because your fuel is empty. This book gives you that faith fuel and a boost to complete your journey.

If it was just about you, it would not matter as much if you quit, but because "Someone's Destiny is Tied to Your Assignment," we are here to help you, and hopefully, you can one day help others. People from all walks of life are experiencing burnout and compassion fatigue, yearning for hope and rejuvenation. I discovered that my unique perspective, derived from my challenges, has set me apart from countless motivational speakers, teachers, preachers, and authors. It was not just the words I spoke or wrote; it was the space from which I spoke and wrote.

This realization propelled me to travel the world, sharing hope through the "I Need a Boost" keynote presentation. Now, the very essence of that address has been transformed into the book you hold in your hands. Its pages are filled with strategies, concepts, tips, and techniques designed to provide the tools you need to increase peace and decrease stress. It offers guidance on finding motivation when you feel drained, staying driven in your purpose while taking time for self-renewal, and navigating life's challenges.

Throughout these pages, I explore profound questions: *When is it time to pivot and embrace change? How do you reignite passion and find renewed energy and motivation? What distinguishes a career from a calling? How can you navigate conflicts and communicate effectively?* I will answer these questions and more, offering practical tools to give you the boost you need for success.

As you embark on this journey, remember that you are not alone. Countless others have faced similar struggles, and we can overcome them together. I hope this book will provide you with the inspiration and guidance you need to rise above challenges, find renewed purpose, and achieve the success you deserve.

CONTENTS

Introduction

"I Need a Boost: What's Driving You Could Be Draining You" is a beacon of light in an overwhelming and exhausting world. In this book, you will discover a powerful resource designed to reignite your spirit, motivate you, and help you navigate the ups and downs of life's journey.

Each chapter has been carefully crafted to tap into the incredible power of words, weaving together encouragement, wisdom, and practical strategies. Through heartfelt anecdotes and thought-provoking exercises, this book aims to awaken your inner strength and remind you of the remarkable potential that lies dormant within.

Imagine the frustration of seeking relief for back pain, only to be told that the solution lies in strengthening your core. That was my experience. I realized I needed assistance from X-rays to MRI scans and, finally, a referral to a sports medicine specialist. Determined to avoid surgery, I was directed towards a ten-week physical therapy program with sessions twice weekly.

To my dismay, my first day of therapy primarily consisted of core exercises. I couldn't help but voice my frustration to the physical therapist, exclaiming that I came here to fix my back, not solely focus on my core. However, her response shed light on a crucial insight: my back was aching due to a weak core. By strengthening my core, I would pave the way for back relief.

This realization got me thinking about the concept of needing a boost. Many people associate burnout with their job, and while that may be a contributing factor, it's not the whole story. By neglecting moments of motivation, relaxation, and downtime, we will leave ourselves drained. Continuously pushing forward without replenishment can lead to burnout, just as I initially overlooked the importance of my core strength in addressing my back pain. Sometimes we ignore what's draining us because we are blinded by the thing that is driving us to be great.

It reminds me of the contest between the older man and the young one to see who could chop down the most trees. The older gentleman took a measured approach, striking the tree once and then resting to sharpen his axe. In contrast, the younger man swung his dull axe relentlessly without taking breaks. Ultimately, the older man achieved more because he recognized the importance of sharpening his tool. This book guides you toward sharpening your tools and rediscovering the essential elements that provide the boost needed to navigate life's challenges.

While the sources of our strength may vary from person to person, we all possess energy reservoirs waiting to be tapped. Some find comfort in their faith, drawing power from their relationship with God and the profound desire to serve the world.

Others may find rejuvenation through their connections with people, their passions, or the pursuit of solving problems and provoking change. Wherever and however your wellspring of strength is located, "I Need a Boost" seeks to become an integral part of your arsenal, providing guidance and support along your unique path.

Our desire is to help you banish self-doubt, embrace possibilities, and take control of your destiny. Let this book be your trusted companion as you embark on a transformative journey toward reigniting your purpose, rediscovering your passion, and rekindling the power within you. Let's illuminate the world with our unwavering light and inspire others to do the same. Remember, the boost you need is within reach.

Join me on this transformative journey as we explore the power of balance and rejuvenation. Together, we will uncover strategies to replenish our energy, find motivation, and embrace the downtime necessary for sustained success. Let's sharpen our axes and equip ourselves with the tools to thrive again in the fight against burnout.

Chapter 1 – Passion Supporting Purpose

Have you ever felt *unmotivated* or *depleted*? Have you ever
questioned your life's work or career? Have you ever wondered if
you selected the right career path? What do you do when you lose
the passion but still have to show up to work every day because
you need the paycheck? What happens if the passion doesn't match
up with what the paycheck offers? Basically, how do you fix the
problem of burnout?

> *Burnout – a state of fatigue or frustration brought
> about by devotion to someone or something that has
> failed to produce the expected reward.*

I Need A Boost

For many people, work can become a mundane and unfulfilling routine; finding motivation and enthusiasm when stuck in an unfulfilling job can be overwhelming.

However, finding meaning and purpose within our professions can make all the difference in how enjoyable and satisfying our jobs become. This chapter will examine strategies for reigniting passion and finding purpose within our professions. These strategies connect to the fact that most people lose their passion when they forget the purpose of the job. So, let's look at an example of this phenomenon with the story of Ms. Velez.

An Educator's Burnout

Ms. Velez had been a teacher for over 15 years, and although she loved teaching, she felt like something was missing. She had lost her passion for the job, and she couldn't figure out why.

One day, as she was grading papers, she came across a document from a student struggling in her class. The student's name was Hanah, and she had written a heartfelt essay about how Ms. Velez had helped her to overcome her fear of speaking in front of others.

Reading Hanah's essay made Ms. Velez remember why she had become a teacher. She had always wanted to make a difference in the lives of her students, but somewhere along the way, she had forgotten her purpose.

As Ms. Velez sat at her desk, she realized she needed a boost to reignite her passion for teaching. She knew she needed to remember her purpose and focus on the impact she was making on her students.

Over the next few weeks, Ms. Velez made an effort to connect with her students on a more personal level. She asked them about their interests and hobbies and even shared some of her own stories with them. Slowly but surely, Ms. Velez began to feel the passion for teaching that she had lost. She realized that her purpose was to teach her students and inspire and motivate them to become the

21

best version of themselves.

With a newfound sense of purpose and passion, Ms. Velez could connect with her students on a deeper level, and she saw a noticeable improvement in their grades and attitudes. Consequently, from that day on, Ms. Velez made a promise to herself to never forget her purpose as a teacher and to always strive to make a positive impact on the lives of her students. She went from singing the popular blues song "The Thrill is Gone" to being inspired by the thought, "I've got my passion back."

> *"If you can't figure out your purpose, figure out your passion. For your passion will lead you right into your purpose." -Bishop T.D. Jakes*

What is your why? Why are you reading this book? Why are you in the field of education? Why do you teach? Why are you in administration? What is your why? You only lose your passion when you forget the purpose! Sometimes we need to remember why!

Did you go into education because you wanted to be a millionaire? Probably not. It has to be something on the inside of you, or another reason other than money, that motivated you to have a career in this field.

Eight Ways to Find Purpose and Passion in Your Work

1. **Connect to your Why.** Consider why you began this job: is it to help people, learn new skills, and provide for your family? Please write it down and revisit this motivation regularly. Make a list of all of the reasons why you selected this field. Are those reasons still relevant, or have they changed over time? Loss of passion typically comes from a lack of purpose. Understanding why you do what you do usually helps with sustaining the desire to do what you do.

2. **Discover Your Strengths and Interests.** Take some time to reflect on the activities and tasks you enjoy, the feedback from your peers, and which projects excite you. Consider how these strengths and interests can be utilized in your current role or whether there are new ones that fit better with them.

3. **Develop a Growth Mindset.** Instead of viewing obstacles and difficulties as setbacks, strive to view them as opportunities to learn and progress. Accept that failure is part of the learning process, and we can develop new skills and strengths by overcoming difficulties.

4. **Connect With Your Colleagues.** Forming relationships with colleagues can give your work life purpose and meaning. Work becomes more enjoyable and satisfying for everyone involved when you come together and strive towards a common goal alongside people you admire and respect.

5. **Pursue a Side Hustle or Hobby.** Sometimes, our day-to-day work doesn't align with our interests and passions. In such cases, pursuing an extracurricular side hustle or hobby that allows us to explore these interests outside of work may be beneficial. Doing so can increase our overall sense of fulfillment and contentment.

6. **Volunteer or Give Back.** Giving back to our communities can be rewarding to find meaning and purpose in our work. Look for opportunities to volunteer or get involved with non-profits or organizations that align with your values and interests.

7. **Take Time Off.** Sometimes, we all need a break to recharge and refocus. Traveling, spending time with loved ones, or pursuing a personal project can help us gain clarity and reignite our enthusiasm for work.

8. **Seek Feedback and Mentorship.** Obtaining feedback from colleagues or seeking mentorship from someone we admire can help us identify areas for growth and

improvement. This provides us with a sense of purpose and motivation as we strive to improve at our jobs.

Three Ways to Maintain Passion

1. **Self-Reflection.** Educators can discover their passions by reflecting on their experiences and values. They might ask themselves questions such as, "What inspired me to become an educator in the first place?" or "What are my core values, and how can they be aligned with my work as an educator?" By answering these questions honestly and thoughtfully, educators gain insight into what drives them and use that insight to inform career decisions and professional growth. Ms. Velez lost her passion, and a letter from a former student brought it back.

2. **Professional Development:** Professional development opportunities can assist educators in discovering and nurturing their passions by giving them new knowledge, skills, and exposure to various teaching methods and approaches. Attending conferences, workshops, or online courses gives educators an edge: they stay abreast of trends and research within their field. Furthermore, educators may seek mentorship or coaching from experienced colleagues who can guide them toward realizing their pursuits.

3. **Work-Life Balance:** Fostering a healthy work-life balance can help educators sustain their passion by preventing burnout and allowing time to pursue hobbies outside of work. They should prioritize self-care activities like exercising, meditation, or spending time with loved ones to recharge and avoid getting overwhelmed. Furthermore, educators can seek out opportunities outside work to pursue interests such as volunteering or participating in community activities that align with their hobbies. By caring for themselves inside and outside the workplace, educators will remain motivated and engaged within their profession.

Conclusion

To find purpose and passion in your work, you need to put in effort and commit to intentional career development. By actively seeking opportunities to explore your interests, you can craft a meaningful and rewarding career that brings you joy and fulfillment. You can reignite your passion for work by reconnecting with your reasons for choosing your career, cultivating a growth mindset, and building strong connections with colleagues. Always remember that it is possible to live a more purposeful and passionate life, even in your work life.

⌐━Key Nugget

Key Nugget for Chapter One: Find the balance between what drives you and what drains you. Recognize that true success is not solely measured by external achievements but also by our internal fulfillment and joy. By aligning actions with passions and remembering our purpose, we can tap into a wellspring of energy and enthusiasm that fuels us rather than depletes us. Understanding why you became an educator and reconnecting with your purpose can reignite your passion and serve as a source of inspiration to drive you even when you feel drained.

Chapter 1 Questions to Ponder

Have You Defined Your Purpose? If not, how can you discover it?

How can you align your purpose with daily activities to increase passion and motivation?

Have you experienced a change in your purpose, and how have you managed it?

Thoughts:

Mansfield Key, III

Chapter 2 – Perception is Key

Working at an alternative school sometimes leaves me exhausted. Sometimes hearing your name called by students repeatedly during the day can become tiring. All day I hear questions like, "*Mr. Key, Mr. Key, can I go to the restroom?*" or "*Mr. Key, Mr. Key, do you think Nick Saban is the best College coach?*" or "*Mr. Key, Mr. Key, do you think Michael Jordon or LeBron James is the goat?*"

Question after question, sometimes from students calling your name over and over – *Mr. Key. Mr. Key* – it can get old. Somedays, I want to hear *my name*, Pete, instead of my work handle, Mr. Key. Have any of you ever felt that way before? Sometimes you need an "escape route.

Speaking of escape routes, *Cheers* was a Television show from the 1980s featuring characters who would go consistently to this bar every night. The last lines in the show's theme song would say, "Wouldn't you like to get away? Sometimes you wanna' go where everybody knows your name, and they're always glad you came...you wanna' be where everybody knows their name."

Are You Willing to Accept Relief?

There was a man who went to see his doctor complaining that something was wrong with his wife. According to the man, she always avoided cooking, cleaning, or being intimate. His physician asked: "Where is she? Is she in the lobby? Go get her." When the man complied, the Doc took the man's wife in his arms, gazed upon her with delight, exclaimed she was beautiful, said she would make an excellent mother and began prancing around with her. At that moment, the man looked at his wife and said, "Doc, I haven't seen that smile in so long." The doctor explained that the wife required encouragement at least four days per week. The guy then said that he went fishing three times weekly and asked if he could bring his wife by the doctor's office so he (the doctor) could give the encouragement his wife needed.

This raises an important question: Are you willing to provide or offer relief when feeling strapped for time? What are your ways of finding relief and rejuvenating yourself when feeling stressed? Do you eat, pray, exercise, or sleep to recharge? Do you balance your needs with the needs of others by offering them relief as well?

Or will you be like the man who found out what his wife needed but chose to delegate to the Doctor instead of doing it himself?

These questions remind me of a time when I was speaking in Delaware recently and met this lady who said, "When the day is done, it doesn't matter what happens – sometimes, one needs a moment to laugh off all stressors." Therefore, it's time for you to take a deep breath, discuss relief options, and take steps toward healing.

POW (Power of Words)

Have you ever considered how powerful words can be? They have an immense effect on our perspectives of the world. If something seems amiss in your world, take time to assess what impact your words are having and ask yourself, "What am I saying?"

Try shifting your perspective when something doesn't sit right with you. Instead of dwelling on the negatives, move toward focusing on the positives. When working in a school system and you witness struggling students while saying to yourself, "This student is getting on my nerves, " try reminding yourself: "I can't wait to put a smile on that child's face!"

Perception is everything. First and foremost, you must see it for yourself before accepting its truth. Secondly, what do you see when looking in the mirror? Every year educators come into contact with students from diverse backgrounds. Some come from homes with two loving parents, while others may live in dangerous circumstances. It is our role as educators to assist each of these students so they may achieve success regardless of any obstacles they may be facing in life.

Life may be difficult at times, and you may feel like giving up. Remember, all humans strive for acceptance, connection, and respect. These are the cornerstones of human interaction and success!

At times the demands of your job can become demanding. I have experience teaching in alternative schools where students vied for my attention, constantly calling out my name while interrupting me mid-thought with questions on topics ranging from sports to politics! While exhausting, this is all part of the job! So, I had to find a way to achieve balance amidst expectations.

How Do You Find Relief?

It would help if you made time for yourself. Find ways to refuel, such as exercise, prayer, or taking deep breaths. Sometimes, all it takes is a laugh to make things right again in a much-needed laugh break!

What you focus on can shape the reality around you, so try

shifting the focus more positively instead of negatively; once that change has taken effect, everything seems brighter!

We tend to rely on our perception of things when making judgments and decisions. However, this can often be inaccurate and misleading.

Confronted by a Snake

One day in the forest, it was an ordinary walk for one man until he came upon an unfamiliar trail where he suddenly found himself face-to-face with a terrifying snake! Startled and terrified, he quickly turned around to flee, anxious with thoughts that the serpent was following him and would continue doing so, no matter how fast he ran. Unfortunately for him, regardless of all escape attempts, he continued to feel pursued.

After running for some time, he was forced to stop and rest his legs because he was so tired. He looked back in fear, only to discover that the snake wasn't following him – it had never left its original spot along the trail! The man was stunned and embarrassed to realize his perception was inaccurate: his fear of snakes had clouded his judgment, leading him to *assume* the worst-case scenario and respond to that assumption.

Perception may not match reality. This story illustrates the power of perception and how it can lead to incorrect conclusions.

Additionally, it emphasizes the necessity of remaining open-minded by not letting our fears or biases cloud our judgment. For effective decisions to be made, we need to see things for what they are and not simply on perception alone.

The Potential for Toxic Perception

> *"When we change the way we look at things, the things we look at will begin to change." -Wayne Dyer*

Perception can be deceivingly powerful. We may perceive ourselves to be reaching burnout when all we require is an extra push forward on our journey. Therefore, we must step back and assess our thoughts and emotions to determine if our perception of the situation is accurate. Are we indeed in danger? Or do we simply need an interlude or a change in pace and direction?

Reminding ourselves that we are not alone is critical when facing difficult times. Everyone faces obstacles, and it is okay to reach out for help or support when necessary, whether consulting with a mentor, confiding in friends, or taking some time alone. It can give us the strength to overcome our obstacles head-on.

As soon as you feel you are burning out or hitting a wall, take a moment to reassess the situation from various perspectives. Are you genuinely burning out or need an additional push? Perceptions can often be misleading; with self-reflection and support, we can find the strength to persevere toward achieving our goals.

Three Things Educators Need to Positively Impact Perception

1. **Empathy:** Educators need to comprehend the challenges their students and coworkers are experiencing daily, which requires empathy. Empathic educators can use their hearts to establish deeper connections with students and coworkers while offering support when necessary. By placing themselves in the shoes of others, educators can better assess what others require from them regarding support, providing tailored approaches tailored toward meeting those needs.

2. **Positive Attitude:** Adopting a positive outlook on work and life can go far in creating an enjoyable learning environment. Teachers who approach their jobs positively tend to inspire and motivate their students and colleagues more readily, helping reduce stress levels and avoid burnout.

3. **Open-mindedness:** As educators, teachers must have an open mind and be willing to listen to various perspectives.

By welcoming different opinions, open-minded educators can foster an inclusive and welcoming learning environment in which every voice is heard and respected. Furthermore, staying current with developments within their field helps educators stay abreast of new trends that can improve teaching techniques and enrich students' learning experiences.

Conclusion

As we conclude the power of perception, it is crucial that we implement the 4 M's to perception: Mind, Mouth, Mood, and Mentality. When a thought hits our mind and words come out of our mouth, that affects our mood, and then, it becomes our mentality. Example: a thought comes that says, *"Today you're tired, and it's going to be a bad day."* It comes out of your mouth, *"I don't feel good. Today is going to be a bad day."* Now the words begin to affect your mood because you thought it and spoke it – now your mood is experiencing it. Once your experience and your mood align, you accept it as a mentality for the day based on perception. Let us begin to speak what we want to see happen instead of what we feel or sense is happening. One of my favorite affirmations is: *I can speak life and cause things to live before they come alive, or I can speak death and cause things to die before they're dead.*

37

I Need A Boost

Life and death are in the power of the tongue, and what we say determines what we see. We have the power to change what happens. Even if we cannot change what happens in that moment, we can change the way we feel or our perception about what happens, as well as how we respond to it. Remember, empathy, open-mindedness, and a positive attitude can impact your perception.

☞Key Nugget

Key Nugget for Chapter Two: Perception is crucial in fueling our passions or draining our energy. As an educator, your perception of your role, your students, and the educational system shapes your daily experiences and influences your well-being. However, the very perceptions that drive your passion and dedication can also be a source to drain you and leave you exhausted. Sometimes we perceive success by things acquired and what others think instead of our authentic definition of success. When we are driven by the need to feel validated, it can lead to us being drained and feeling a sense of emptiness. Examining and adjusting your perspectives can transform what is draining you into something that empowers you.

Chapter 2 Questions To Ponder

How can we overcome negative self-perceptions to boost confidence and outlook?

What techniques can you use to change your perspective and understand situations from multiple viewpoints?

How can you cultivate positive impressions of others and foster more meaningful relationships?

Thoughts:

Chapter 3 – The Four R's of Relationship

How can we build meaningful and genuine relationships in today's fast-paced social media world? With social media becoming essential for professional success, building healthy relationships has never been more necessary in life. By making meaningful connections that benefit you professionally, personally, and networking-wise, building authentic relationships has never been more essential. They help advance careers, gain new clients, expand networks, and build a system of new contacts. They also go well beyond amassing followers on social media or collecting business cards - it means making genuine connections which, in turn, can assist others by helping themselves. This chapter will discuss examples related to the Four R's of authentic relationships:

41

relatability, reliability, relevance, and realness.

Going Nappy for My Students

One day as I entered one of the schools I work at, one of my students approached me and said: "Mr. Key, I bet you won't go nappy on purpose?" When they said this, I replied with, 'Yes I will!" However, I was looking confused. So, another student described what "nappy on purpose" meant! They explained it as taking a sponge and rolling it over your hair until it looks nappy and curly.

I called my barber and told him to change my style to NOP – Nappy on Purpose. So, the following week, when I revisited my barber, I requested he adjust it accordingly. And when I walked back into class the next week, the students said, "Oh, Mr. Key! Yes, sir, I see you – yes, sir! You got it." Then he looked at me and said, "You did that well for us, but I bet when you get on one of those big stages, you won't do it like that." I replied, "Yes, I will!"

At that moment, I realized it wasn't just about hair; instead, it was about steps to build relationships with students. While getting tattoos or wearing certain clothes may help form bonds between teachers and their pupils, it might also seem extreme to some. So, what are you willing to do to connect? Our subjects in the seats are as important as what we teach.

I am not recommending getting tattoos or changing your dress or shoes or even hair to connect with your students, but I am suggesting this – find a way to connect. The famous quote, "They don't care how much you know until they know how much you care," is true. So, what can you do to show you care?

Mr. Williams Connects with His Students

Meet Mr. Williams, a high school math teacher. who loves teaching but sometimes needs help to connect with his students, particularly those who are more preoccupied with phones than learning algebra.

Mr. Williams overheard some students discussing the latest Marvel movie. To his delight, they seemed just as enthusiastic about its impending release as he was, so he saw an opportunity to connect with his students in a unique but authentic way.

Mr. Williams decided to incorporate Marvel characters such as Iron Man and Spider-Man in his classroom lessons, using Iron Man to explain linear equations and Spider-Man to demonstrate geometric principles. His students were intrigued and engaged, prompting them to ask more questions and participate more freely during class, so much so that Mr. Williams created a bulletin board featuring Marvel-related artwork by his students.

By finding common ground and sharing his interests with his

students, he was able to foster a more engaging learning environment – plus, they got to geek out over Marvel together!

It's essential to consider your students' needs and preferences when setting up an engaging learning experience. Here are some ways to show how much we care.

Five Strategies for Establishing Genuine Relationships

> *"Rules & Regulation without relationship leads to rebellion and rejection" -Josh McDowell*

1. **Be True.** Don't try to be someone you aren't; students can tell when you're trying too hard, which can come across as inauthentic. Instead, embrace your quirks and unique personality to make yourself more relatable; not everyone has to look or act just like their students to establish connections. Mr. Williams made himself more accessible by celebrating what made him special, which helped strengthen relationships among his pupils.

2. **Establish Common Ground.** Explore what topics or subjects your students find most fascinating, such as sports, video games, or fashion. Use their interests as part of your

lessons for greater engagement. One professor I know uses a concept called 2x10. This is a formula to help educators relate to students better. The concept is to take two minutes every day over ten days to connect with the same student. Simply asking open-ended questions related to that student's interests is enough to create a bond and make them feel cared for and special!

3. **Be Reliable:** Be prompt, well prepared, and adhere to any agreements made. Students value consistency and reliability as much as anything, especially in our chaotic world. Make sure your teaching connects directly to their daily lives in some way.

4. **Stay Relevant:** Stay up to date with current trends and technologies so that your students know you are willing to adapt to meet their needs. Staying relevant allows your teachings to connect to something happening today that enhances learning.

5. **Be Receptive to Feedback:** Ask your students for their input on your teaching style and anyway you could enhance it. While every suggestion won't apply directly, showing that you value their opinions can go a long way toward building strong relationships between teachers and students.

Three Components of Strong Relationships in Education:

1. **Active Listening.** This involves paying close attention to what the other person is saying, asking clarifying questions, and responding thoughtfully. When educators practice active listening with their students and colleagues, it demonstrates respect for their perspectives and opinions, fosters trust, and establishes rapport between themselves and students or colleagues alike. Furthermore, active listening provides educators with insights into the needs or challenges faced by either side, which may inform instructional practices and professional collaborations.

2. **Authenticity.** Educators who are authentic and genuine when engaging with students and colleagues tend to build stronger relationships. Authenticity requires honesty about one's strengths and weaknesses by acknowledging mistakes, showing vulnerability when appropriate, and taking time to know students individually. This builds connections based on shared interests or experiences.

3. **Collaboration.** Educators who collaborate with their students and colleagues develop stronger relationships by working towards shared goals. Collaboration involves the following: listening to and respecting the ideas and contributions of others, sharing expertise and resources, and working towards mutually beneficial results. When

educators collaborate with their colleagues, they form supportive professional communities that encourage continuous learning and growth. When they collaborate with students, educators empower students to take ownership of their knowledge, foster the development of teamwork skills, and build problem-solving abilities.

Conclusion

Teaching is about more than simply imparting knowledge – it is also about building meaningful relationships. By remaining true to yourself, identifying common ground, being reliable, staying relevant, and accepting feedback openly from students, you can form genuine bonds that help them learn and grow as individuals - you may make some new Marvel fans along the way! Remember, using humor and personality will have a lasting effect on them!

🔑 Key Nugget

Key Nugget for Chapter Three: Being relatable, reliable, relevant, and real reminds us that we are not alone. Connection provides a sense of belonging and validation while fostering a sense of security, enabling us to lean on each other during difficult times and celebrate together during moments of success.

Chapter 3 Questions To Ponder

How can you ensure your actions and communication are relatable, reliable, relevant, and authentic?

How can these principles be integrated into personal and professional relationships?

How can you increase impact and effectiveness at work or within your community?

Thoughts:

I Need A Boost

Chapter 4 – Conflict & Communication

Conflict is an inevitable part of any workplace. However, when handled properly, conflicts can be resolved and become opportunities for growth and learning. Good communication skills are essential in managing workplace conflicts and building strong relationships with coworkers, and they can help prevent conflicts from escalating. In this chapter, we will discuss strategies for navigating conflict and improving communication in the workplace.

Workplace Conflict Between John and Sarah

Sarah and her coworker John had been butting heads for weeks while working on a new project. Sarah felt John was not contributing equally to the project and did not take her suggestions seriously. On the other hand, John felt that Sarah was micromanaging him and not respecting his ideas.

Sarah decided to schedule a meeting with John to discuss their issues and devise a plan to move forward. During the meeting, they both had the opportunity to express their concerns and listen to the other person's perspective. By actively listening to each other, they could find common ground and come up with a solution that worked for both of them. They also set clear expectations for how they would work together in the future and regularly checked in to ensure they were both on track.

Four Ways to Navigate Conflict and Communication

> *"Conflict challenges us to listen with empathy, speak with clarity, and seek common ground through effective communication." -Unknown*

1. **Listening.** Listening involves hearing the words someone is saying, understanding their perspective, and showing empathy. By doing so, you can gain insights into their

emotions, needs, and motivations, which can help you respond more constructively. For example, suppose you are a manager having a difficult conversation with an employee who has been consistently missing deadlines. By listening to their explanation, you may find that they are struggling with a personal issue affecting their work performance. Rather than reprimanding them, you can work with them to find a solution that addresses their needs while also meeting the company's needs.

2. **Find Common Ground.** Conflict often arises because people have different perspectives, interests, and priorities. However, by finding common ground, you can create a shared understanding that can lead to more productive communication and collaboration. For instance, suppose you are part of a team working on a project with a tight deadline. You may have different opinions on approaching the project, but you all share the same goal of completing it on time. By focusing on this shared goal, you can work together to find a solution that considers everyone's ideas and strengths.

3. **Be Respectful.** Respect is a crucial element of effective communication, particularly in the workplace. By treating coworkers with respect, you can create a positive work environment where everyone feels valued and appreciated. For example, suppose you are in a meeting with a coworker

presenting an idea you disagree with. Rather than dismissing their idea outright, you can acknowledge their perspective and provide constructive feedback. This approach shows that you respect their input and are willing to work with them to find a solution that works for everyone.

4. **Communicate Effectively.** Effective communication is essential in any workplace setting, and it involves using language that is clear, concise, and free of assumptions. By communicating effectively, you can ensure your message is understood and avoid misunderstandings that can lead to conflict. For instance, suppose you are part of a team working on a new project. If you are unsure, asking questions and seeking clarification is essential. By doing so, you can ensure that everyone is on the same page and that the project is progressing smoothly. Additionally, avoiding making assumptions and using precise language can help prevent misunderstandings leading to conflict.

Conclusion

Conflict and miscommunication are common in any workplace setting. However, by implementing these four strategies, you can navigate conflict more effectively, improve communication, and create a more positive work environment for yourself and your colleagues.

The Coin

One man stared at his side of the coin while making his case that he saw heads. The gentleman on the other side disagreed, saying, "You cannot see heads because I see tails." Both men began to express their point of view. The gentleman looking at heads said the other man couldn't see tails because he was holding the coin and looking directly at heads on the coin. The other man continues to argue that the coin can only be tails. Finally, they agreed to turn the coin around so both men could see what the other one was seeing. They were looking at the same coin that held the same value but viewed it from two different sides.

Sometimes conflict is just two people looking at the same issue from two different sides. The student sees it from their perspective, and the teacher sees it from theirs. The principal looks at the same situation from another point of view. The Parent or the Superintendent can look at the same situation from another point of view. This is why it's also helpful to address conflicts head-on rather than letting them fester and escalate. Let's look at another example that demonstrates this point.

Ms. Johnson's Disruptive Student

Ms. Johnson noticed that one of her students, Jimmy, was consistently disruptive in class and often caused conflicts with his classmates. Despite her best efforts to address the issue in class and through one-on-one conversations with Jimmy, the behavior continued to escalate.

Ms. Johnson realized that she needed to address the conflict head-on and promptly before it had a further negative impact on the class. She met with Jimmy's parents and the school counselor to discuss the issue and find a solution together.

During the meeting, Ms. Johnson was direct and honest about the behavior she had observed and its impact on the class. She also listened carefully to Jimmy's parents and the counselor who provided valuable insights into Jimmy's home life and personal struggles.

Together, they developed a plan to support Jimmy and address the underlying issues causing his disruptive behavior. This included providing additional academic and emotional support and involving Jimmy's parents in his education and behavior management.

By addressing the conflict head-on and on time, Ms. Johnson was able to prevent it from escalating further and creating a more severe issue for the school and the students. Her direct communication and willingness to work collaboratively with Jimmy's parents and the school counselor helped to find a solution that supported Jimmy's well-being and academic success.

This story highlights the importance of being direct and timely when addressing conflicts, particularly in a school environment where the well-being and education of students are at stake. By communicating effectively and working collaboratively, Ms. Johnson was able to improve the situation and create a positive outcome for all involved.

Three Ways Educators Resolve Conflict between Colleagues

1. **Seek to understand:** When conflicts arise, listening actively to the other person's point of view is essential. Try to understand their perspective, even if you disagree with it. Ask open-ended questions to clarify their position and avoid making assumptions or jumping to conclusions. Active listening can help you gain insight into the other person's motivations and feelings, which can be essential for finding a resolution.

2. **Communicate clearly and respectfully:** Clear and respectful communication is critical in resolving conflicts.

Use "I" statements to express your thoughts and feelings and avoid blaming or accusing the other person. Be mindful of your tone and body language, as these can influence how your message is received. Remember to stay focused on the issue and avoid getting sidetracked by personal attacks or unrelated topics.

3. **Seek a neutral third party.** Sometimes, despite your best efforts, conflicts can be challenging to resolve. In these cases, seeking a neutral third party to mediate the dispute can be helpful. This could be a supervisor, a mentor, or a professional mediator. A neutral third party can provide an objective perspective and help facilitate a productive dialogue between the parties involved. Conflict resolution requires patience, empathy, and a willingness to work toward a mutually acceptable solution. Educators can successfully resolve personal and professional conflicts by actively listening, communicating clearly and respectfully, and seeking a neutral third party.

Conclusion

Conflict is an inevitable part of any workplace, but it can also be an opportunity for growth and learning. By addressing conflicts directly, actively listening, finding common ground, being respectful, and communicating effectively, you can navigate workplace conflicts and improve communication in your workplace. Remember, creating a positive and supportive working environment can ultimately lead to improved outcomes and job satisfaction for everyone involved.

⚲Key Nugget

Key Nugget for Chapter Four: Are you aware of the driving forces behind your conflicts? Are these driving forces draining your energy and hindering constructive resolutions? By understanding the connection between what drives you and how it can drain you, you can empower yourself to navigate conflicts more effectively, preserve your energy, and foster healthier, more fulfilling relationships. Remember, conflict can be an opportunity for growth and understanding when approached with self-awareness and empathy. By examining what's driving you and recognizing how it could be draining you, you can transform conflicts into catalysts for positive change.

Chapter 4 Questions to Ponder

How can you approach conflict resolution constructively and productively?

Which communication techniques can help de-escalate tension-filled situations and foster understanding?

And finally, how can you balance assertiveness and empathy to produce positive outcomes?

Thoughts:

Chapter 5 - Making A Difference

In this chapter, we will jump right into a series of stories that make specific points related to making a difference.

Mr. Lee's Principal Power

Mr. Lee was an educator brimming with passion who believed intensely in making an impactful difference in his students' lives. He aimed to inspire his pupils with the love of learning. Finally, this dream came true when he was appointed principal at the local high school.

Mr. Lee was keen to make an impressive first impression as the principal of his school and was determined to create an inclusive environment for his students and staff. To do this, he implemented new programs and initiatives designed to improve his pupils' academic performance and provide a safe space where all pupils could feel welcome regardless of background or socio-economic status.

Mr. Lee struggled to make an impactful difference at his school, as none of his initiatives seemed to resonate with students or staff members. Mr. Lee needed help understanding why his efforts didn't have their desired impact and became increasingly frustrated. One day, Mr. Lee decided to talk with one of his senior teachers to seek advice. The teacher carefully listened to Mr. Lee's concerns before explaining that to make a difference truly, he needed to understand students' and staffers' needs and priorities before creating new programs or initiatives.

Mr. Lee followed his teacher's advice and built relationships with his students and staff, listened carefully to their concerns and needs, and worked collaboratively to create a positive and inclusive school culture. Soon enough, Mr. Lee began seeing significant differences within his school; students became more engaged in learning while staff became more accepting of the change.

Mr. Lee realized, despite his best efforts, that he needed help to make a significant impact; he needed the support and collaboration of students and staff members alike to have any effect. Making a difference requires patience, persistence, listening to others' perspectives, and being willing to learn from others' experiences. Mr. Lee realized that making an impactful difference wasn't about creating new programs or initiatives but building relationships, encouraging collaboration, and creating an inclusive culture that allowed students and staff alike to thrive in an inviting and safe environment. Though his impact wasn't what was initially desired, Mr. Lee knew he had made an impression on many individuals within his school district by creating safe environments in which all could flourish.

Mrs. Cook's Example of Belief & Connection

Mrs. Cook was a public high school principal in a low-income community. Mrs. Cook had an immense passion for education, believing that every student, no matter their background, had an equal potential to succeed. To create an atmosphere conducive to productivity, she understood it was imperative to build relationships, promote positive school culture and deliver effective instructional leadership.

Mrs. Cook made it a point to build positive relationships by greeting each student by name upon entering school each morning and getting to know her staff, asking about their interests and listening to their ideas for improvement. By creating strong bonds among her members, Mrs. Cook fostered an environment where all felt valued and respected.

Mrs. Cook took steps to foster a positive school culture by setting clear expectations for behavior and academic performance, encouraging her staff to model these expectations themselves through continuous improvement practices, celebrating success while encouraging creativity and innovation within her classroom, and offering professional development opportunities for her staff. She did this while also understanding that investing in them would ultimately benefit her students.

Mrs. Cook recognized the impact that belief has on students and staff, especially when it came to effective instructional leadership and improving student outcomes by creating an enjoyable learning experience. Therefore, she supported and guided her teachers in their instructional practices.

To do this, she provided resources and support for professional development; additionally, she implemented programs that helped develop essential life skills like leadership development and career readiness among her students. Effective instructional leadership was paramount in improving student outcomes and creating a positive educational experience for her pupils.

Under Mrs. Cook's leadership, school culture improved significantly. Students became more engaged with learning while teachers felt inspired to instruct. Furthermore, everyone felt valued and respected at school. Mrs. Cook's commitment to her students and staff paid off in spades. Students who previously struggled in school were now graduating and entering college; teachers who once felt disengaged were directly inspired and enthusiastic. All because Mrs. Cook demonstrated the power of connection and belief through simple acts like greeting her students by name and building relationships. This type of impact was a crucial key to her success.

Three Ways to Make a Difference with Students

> *"Making a difference is not about the magnitude of your actions, but the intention and impact they have on others."*
> *-Unknown*

1. **Get to Know Your Students.** Make time to get to know each student by asking about their interests, hobbies, and extra curriculum activities. Listen carefully and show genuine curiosity for what's going on in their lives; by doing this, you will build trust and form bonds between yourself and students.

2. **Show Empathy and Understanding:** Students want to feel understood, and educators can make a difference by showing empathy and understanding when students struggle. Acknowledging their challenges while offering support and

guidance will demonstrate to students that you care about them as individuals and invest in their success.

3. **Cultivate a Positive Classroom Environment:** Cultivating a welcoming and inclusive space where students feel free to express themselves is critical in building relationships with students. Celebrating their accomplishments and offering constructive criticism helps them improve. When students feel supported and valued, their engagement increases significantly, and their motivation for learning grows substantially.

Three Bonus Tips for Making a Difference

*   **Cultivate Positive Relationships,** In the story shared at the beginning of this chapter, we see that Mr. Lee took the time to get to know both teachers and students. He listened attentively when they shared concerns or ideas, offered support when needed, and showed appreciation. Making people feel valued will motivate and engage them fully in their work.

*   **Foster a Positive School Culture,** Create a welcoming and encouraging school culture that recognizes diversity, celebrates accomplishments, encourages creativity and innovation, and sets clear expectations for behavior and

academic performance. Make sure to model these expectations yourself while providing opportunities for professional growth and celebrating success.

- **Provide Effective Instructional Leadership.** Guide your teachers in their instructional practices, providing resources and support for professional development. Effective classroom teachers create positive learning experiences for their students that improve outcomes while creating a culture of continuous improvement.

Conclusion

For leaders in the school system (such as principals and administrators), actions speak louder than words. They must show students and staff the values they hold through positive modeling of behavior and values while inspiring them to follow in your footsteps. By listening, fostering positivity, and providing effective leadership, leaders can make a significant, impactful contribution to their school's community. As a school principal, adding value to your community is integral to building a thriving school culture. Follow these simple tips while remembering to have some fun along the way - laughter can be medicine in this regard!

⚷ Key Nugget

Key Nugget for Chapter Five: Emotions are often the key that pushes people to make a change – or what we know as making a difference. Using emotions as inspiration, you can quote the "I'M MAD" mantra to remind you of this key nugget. I-M-M-A-D stands for "I Must Make A Difference." Educators who are driven by their passion to make a difference in the lives of their students could also be drained by the effort it takes to support their students. Pursuing quality education, nurturing young minds, and making a lasting impact can be both fulfilling and exhausting. As an educator, your drive to create a positive learning environment and inspire your students may sometimes lead to immense pressure and self-imposed expectations. By recognizing and embracing your limitations, you can relieve the continuous pressure and the lingering feeling as if you're never doing enough.

Chapter 5 Questions to Ponder

What small steps can you take to make a difference in your community or the world?

How can you leverage your skills and talents to contribute to a cause you care about?

How can you measure the results of your efforts to optimize their effectiveness?

Thoughts:

Chapter 6 - Motivation And Energy

Have you ever needed more energy to complete a simple task? Have you ever needed help finding the motivation to get up each morning or take on new projects at work? If this sounds familiar, don't despair: many people face similar difficulties occasionally. Still, there are ways you can overcome not having energy and motivation and give yourself the boost necessary for success.

Step one in finding motivation and energy is understanding their importance. That's one of the factors necessary for reaching personal or professional goals successfully. With the right level of motivation, it is easier to stay on course; with energy, it's possible to move forward or take necessary actions.

Why do we feel depleted and lack motivation? There can be numerous causes for this feeling, such as stress, lack of sleep, poor nutrition, and an inactive lifestyle. If we neglect ourselves in these ways, we risk leaving ourselves depleted and short on the enthusiasm needed for an active life!

You can take simple steps to increase your motivation and energy levels. For example, getting enough sleep, eating healthy, exercising regularly, managing your stress effectively, surrounding yourself with positive influences, and setting achievable goals that you can celebrate. All this will help to maintain a positive perspective and remain motivated!

If you need an extra boost, don't despair: with hard work and determination, you can find the motivation and energy necessary for success. By taking care of yourself and remaining focused on your goals, you will easily overcome any hurdles to win and reach success.

Ms. Thompson Gets Re-Energized

Ms. Thompson was always a hard-working superintendent, but her demanding job started to affect her. She was constantly overwhelmed with work and unable to achieve a work-life balance. Her motivation and energy were fading away. It became difficult to meet the high demands placed on her by her job. Finally, she realized she had to find a way to increase her motivation and energy. She realized if she didn't, she would become more overwhelmed and depleted. Ms. Thompson felt the pressures of her staff, her students, the school board, and the community. She also found it difficult to please everyone.

Ms. Thompson started by focusing her attention on healthy habits and self-care. She ensured she slept enough, ate a nutritious and balanced diet, and exercised regularly. She also used mindfulness meditation to decrease stress and increase focus. As a result, her productivity began to increase.

Ms. Thompson went further by also setting boundaries to maintain a healthy balance between work and life. She spent quality time with family and disconnected from work regularly. These practices allowed her to regain motivation and energy and excel in her position as school superintendent. She made a significant difference in the lives of both students and teachers while maintaining her well-being. It's important to prioritize self-care and establish healthy habits to reduce stress, increase motivation and boost energy.

Ms. Thompson's story is a clear example of burnout. It's easy for educators to feel overwhelmed by the demands of their job. Burnout takes away energy for tasks like lesson planning, grading, managing a class, and meeting students' needs. Ms. Thompson lived by the slogan, "Always doing right by kids and adults benefits families and the community." Let's look at a story of someone who never lost their momentum.

Ms. Rodriguez Maintains Her Energy

As an experienced educator like Ms. Rodriguez, staying motivated and energized had become a top priority. She understood that to be successful, she had to put herself first. Ms. Rodriguez began by setting realistic goals for herself. She prioritized her daily tasks and made a list. She could concentrate on the tasks that needed to be completed while avoiding stress. Ms. Rodriguez took breaks frequently throughout the day to maintain her energy level. She would walk, stretch, or close her eyes to breathe deeply.

The short breaks refreshed her mind and prevented fatigue. Ms. Rodriguez made time to care for herself outside of her work. She had hobbies such as painting and hiking that allowed her to recharge. Ms. Rodriguez found the motivation and energy she needed to avoid burnout by prioritizing her care, setting realistic goals, and taking frequent breaks. She was passionate about her job as an educator, and she had a positive influence on her students' lives.

Three Ways to Stay Energized and Motivated

> *"Motivation is the spark that ignites action, and energy is the fuel that keeps the fire burning." -Unknown*

1. **Exercise Regularly.** Physical activity has many positive health and well-being benefits, including increasing energy levels, decreasing stress levels, and overall wellness benefits. Consume A Nutritious Diet: Eating has also been proven to increase energy levels while contributing to overall well-being.

2. **Disconnect From Work.** Establish boundaries and take time away from work to create a healthy work-life balance. Spend time with family and friends, pursue hobbies or interests, or relax to recharge your batteries.

3. **Take Action Towards Recovery.** Reach out for assistance from colleagues, mentors, or counselors to manage stress and maintain overall well-being.

Three Mistakes Leading to Poor Motivation

1. **Neglecting Your Self-Care.** People may place work responsibilities before their well-being. This causes them to neglect necessary self-care practices such as exercise, healthy eating, and hobbies to relax or relieve stress. This also increases stress levels and burnout, which would reduce their overall effectiveness in assigned roles.

2. **Failure to Establish Boundaries.** Some people may find it challenging to balance work responsibilities with personal life, which can add an extra layer of strain and increase stress. This type of burnout makes it hard for them to unwind between shifts. Not setting clear boundaries between work and personal time may increase pressure as they struggle to decompress properly in their free time and recharge themselves properly.

3. **Failing to Seek Support.** People may feel as though they must handle everything themselves. Therefore, they avoid seeking support from colleagues, mentors, or counselors out of fear that reaching out is shameful. This causes stress levels to increase, and once again – it leads to burnout. This particular burnout is the result of rejecting the resources that help manage energy effectively, creating unnecessary strain.

Conclusion

For educators to remain healthy and effective, prioritizing stress relief and creating habits that foster success is paramount. Motivation and energy are always necessary, especially for responsibilities like leading a district successfully or inspiring students. Mindfulness practices, exercise regimens, healthy eating, and supportive resources are just some of the ways to preserve and maximize the energy that educators need. It is crucial for educators to prioritize and cultivate their self-care so they can be at their best for both themselves and others.

Key Nugget

Key Nugget for Chapter Six: By aligning your daily actions with your underlying values and goals, you can regain a sense of fulfillment and combat the draining effects of external pressures. Educators often put the needs of their students above their own, neglecting their physical, emotional, and mental well-being. When you recognize what is driving you could be draining you, then you can begin to implement strategies to maintain motivation and energy.

Chapter 6 Questions to Ponder

What actions can be taken to maintain motivation and energy throughout the day?

List any bad habits or behaviors that drain your energy and motivation.

How can you eliminate or reduce them?

List any suggestions or techniques that can be used to boost your motivation and energy in your daily life.

Thoughts:

Chapter 7 – Personal Development

Teaching can be challenging at times. Personal development is essential to staying enthusiastic, practical, and passionate about education. In this chapter, we will examine why educators should prioritize personal growth to address professional issues while remaining motivated.

Let's start with a story about Ms. Johnson to see how a person can maintain enthusiasm and effectiveness throughout their career by pursuing personal growth.

Ms. Johnson's Continuous Education

Ms. Johnson noticed that her enthusiasm and energy were waning as the demands took away time from personal and professional development. She was also dealing with compassion fatigue and burnout. Ms. Johnson decided to prioritize attending professional workshops and conferences since she found them to be both fun and educational.

The conferences and workshops provided her with innovative teaching methods and new strategies for engaging her students, and new ways to teach. She also kept a journal of reflections on her teaching and the areas where she needed to improve.

Through her personal development journey, Ms. Johnson discovered project-based and new, improved classroom strategies, which she has implemented in her classes. She also supported her personal development with yoga and meditation classes. Now, she sees personal development as a must and continues to prioritize it in her career.

Five Ways to Support Professional Development

> *"Professional development is not just about acquiring new skills; it's about expanding your mindset, broadening your horizons, and embracing a growth-oriented approach."*
> *-Unknown*

In chapter six, we discussed the importance of self-care. Another benefit of self-care is that it can also support professional development. Here are some self-care practices that can enhance your continued education and improvement.

1. **Reflection & Feedback.** A reflective journal or a feedback group can assist teachers in recognizing areas for improvement and creates innovative teaching strategies. Reflection also allows educators to assess their strengths and weaknesses as teachers and devise plans for self-improvement.

2. **Mutual Support.** Seeking assistance from colleagues or professional counselors can provide an enabling atmosphere when discussing teaching challenges or

exploring strategies for personal growth. Seeking assistance should not be seen as a sign of weakness but as an essential part of personal and professional growth and development.

3. **Maintenance of Self-Care Activities**. Educators who engage in self-care for their energy and motivation should be aware that they also support their professional development. This is further motivation for maintaining habits like exercise, mindfulness, meditation, and hobbies.

4. **Practice Gratitude**. Teaching can often become challenging; therefore, taking the time each day to reflect on all you are grateful for can change your perspective and restore the joy in teaching. A daily gratitude journal or simply making sure to spend time thinking about all you appreciate can bring back a more positive outlook and renewed joy for education.

5. **Establish Connections:** Teaching can often feel isolating, so having connections is necessary to remain supported and motivated. Joining teacher's groups or attending networking events provides opportunities to share ideas, discuss challenges and successes with fellow educators, form meaningful bonds among colleagues, and supportive communities to help you get through any tough day.

Conclusion

Personal development is an ongoing process that helps teachers manage professional issues and remain motivated in their roles. By attending professional development workshops, reflecting on teaching practice, practicing self-care techniques, and seeking support, they can stay inspired and effective at their jobs. Investing in yourself will give you greater confidence, increase your qualifications, and help you increase your fulfillment as an educator.

# Key Nugget

Key Nugget for Chapter Seven: It's essential to have a clear understanding of your aspirations, strengths, and areas for growth. Setting realistic and meaningful goals allows you to channel your drive in productive ways and avoid the drain of aimless striving. It's important to pace yourself and avoid getting caught up in the perfectionism trap. While it is natural to want to excel and constantly improve, the pressure to be flawless can become overwhelming. Investing in professional development, pursuing hobbies, cultivating relationships, and prioritizing self-care activities that recharge your energy and keep you driven instead of drained are one of the keys to longevity in the educational field.

Chapter 7 Questions to Ponder

What steps should you take to further advance professionally?

How can personal development enhance your performance?

What areas could you benefit from further personal development?

Thoughts:

Chapter 8 - Being Adaptable to Change

Education constantly shifts due to curriculum changes, technological developments, and student demands. Teachers must adapt and adjust to changing methods and change with the times. This chapter explores the significance of educators and ways to further develop their abilities.

Mrs. Ramirez's Transformation

Mrs. Ramirez had been teaching the same curriculum for several years when suddenly, her school introduced a new math program. This new program required her to introduce new concepts and embrace different teaching methods. Though initially feeling discomfort by this change in approach to teaching, Mrs. Ramirez eventually recognized its significance and appreciated how important it would be in shaping her teaching methods and strategies.

Mrs. Ramirez began by attending professional development workshops that addressed the new math program and collaborating with other teachers to devise effective teaching strategies. Furthermore, she sought feedback from students and used their suggestions to adapt her instruction accordingly. Mrs. Ramirez adjusted to the new mathematics program through her hard work and efforts, leading her students to greater engagement and academic success in their studies. We can learn from Mrs. Ramirez and her adaptability.

Five Ways to Adopt a Flexible & Adaptable Attitude

> *"One reason people resist change is because they focus on what they have to give up instead of what they have to gain." -Rick Godwin*

For some, adaptability isn't something that can simply be commanded or easily adopted. Preparation is required. Here are five ways to build an adaptable and flexible attitude.

1. **Acknowledge Change.** Acknowledging change in education is inevitable and should be used to enhance teaching and student learning.

2. **Attend Professional Development Workshops**. Keep abreast of emerging methods, technologies, and student needs by attending workshops. Attending workshops prepares you for upcoming changes and keeps you current.

3. **Collaborate With Colleagues**. Exchange teaching strategies and ideas with colleagues and collaborate on projects and lesson plans. To help you avoid the rut of repetition, it will help you see a different perspective.

4. **Solicit Feedback From Students**. Consider student views regarding their learning experiences. Their feedback encourages you to consistently tailor your approach to the unique components of each class.

5. **Be Open to New Ideas**. Be ready and willing to experiment with various teaching methods, technologies, and strategies; be receptive to feedback from colleagues and students; always welcome suggestions or criticism that arises that can be helpful.

Conclusion

Flexibility and adaptability are invaluable skills for teachers looking to navigate change and enhance student learning successfully. By accepting changes, attending professional development workshops, working collaboratively with colleagues, soliciting student feedback, and remaining open-minded to new ideas, educators can hone these abilities further and foster engaging learning environments for their pupils. While being flexible requires effort and practice, its rewards in terms of student success and personal satisfaction are immense. Here's a mantra to encourage this adaptability through an acronym known as **E.R.A:**

E - Embrace new ideas and technologies.

R - Remain open-minded and responsive to feedback.

A - Adapt, Adjust, and be Acceptant of the process.

# Key Nugget

Key Nugget for Chapter Eight: Sometimes, the fear that comes with transformation keeps us from making the necessary changes for success. It is said that people fear change because they are more focused on what they have to give up rather than what they have to gain. Change can be uncomfortable and challenging, triggering doubts and uncertainties. Remember, embracing transformation is not just about adapting to external changes but also nurturing your growth and well-being. By understanding the potential draining effects of your drive and taking proactive steps to maintain balance and self-care, you can continue making a profound impact as an educator while sustaining your motivation and fulfillment. What drives you to seek change?

Chapter 8 Questions to Ponder

How do you personally react and embrace change or unexpected challenges?

What strategies have you developed to adapt and succeed under changing conditions?

How can you develop a more adaptable mindset to navigate uncertainty?

Thoughts:

Chapter 9 - Fulfilling Your Calling

Teaching is more than a job; it's a calling that demands a deep commitment to positively impacting students' lives. To reach your full potential as an educator, your work must align with your mission and purpose. We will explore ways you can fulfill that calling in this chapter.

In previous chapters, we used stories to introduce the concepts to be learned. But in this chapter, we will focus on simple reminders about the true impact of being an educator.

The Deeper Meaning of Being a Teacher

Teachers do more than just educate. They shape the future, inspire others, and influence lives.

- **Shapers of Tomorrow.** Teachers play an invaluable role in shaping future leaders, innovators, and problem solvers. Their education can significantly shape our collective future, making their work valuable to society.

- **Inspire Others.** By making a difference in students' lives, exceptional and dedicated educators can inspire other individuals to pursue careers in education, creating a positive ripple effect within society's educational system and building brighter futures for all.

- **The Power to Influence Lives.** Teachers influence, impact, and inspire students from all walks of life. By fulfilling your calling as a teacher and aligning your work with your mission and purpose, you can make an enduring mark on society by shaping your students' lives while leaving an imprint of your own.

Five Ways to Maintain and Enhance Your Calling

> *"The true fulfillment of a teacher's calling lies not in the applause or recognition, but in the profound impact they have on the lives of their students, and the legacy they leave behind."* -Unknown

1. **Reflect on Your Values and Mission.** To ensure your work aligns with your mission and purpose, it is essential to reflect on the values and missions guiding your teaching experience. How well does teaching align with your values? How has this impacted the way you teach? Through taking time for self-reflection, teachers can more successfully incorporate their mission and values into their work, leading to more fulfilling experiences as teachers!

2. **Unleash Your Passions.** Integrating your interests and passions into teaching can boost productivity while simultaneously engaging students. By integrating them with your lessons, you can make work more satisfying for yourself and the students involved.

3. **Establish Strong Relationships with Students and Families.**

We must create an inviting and welcoming atmosphere for both our students and their families to form meaningful bonds between both. Showing our care for their success – by prioritizing these relationships – will allow for more fulfilling experiences for us.

4. **Develop Your Skills.** Consistently seeking opportunities that align with your mission and purpose as an educator (through conferences, workshops, or online courses) is critical to continuing professional growth and making an impactful difference in students' lives. When you make an effort to develop your teaching abilities further, you have more impact on your students!

5. **Assume Challenges and Explore New Experiences.** Pushing yourself out of your comfort zone (and accepting new challenges) will enable you to grow and help you achieve a connection between your work and your mission. By being open to new experiences and opportunities, you can continue making an impactful difference while fulfilling your calling.

Conclusion

As an educator, you have an unparalleled chance to shape students' lives and help them unlock their full potential. Your guidance, support, and encouragement could make all the difference for someone working toward specific career goals or facing personal hardship. Zig Ziglar always said, "Your career is what you're paid to do, and your calling is what you were made to do." While a career may provide stability and financial rewards, a calling provides a profound sense of purpose and fulfillment that transcends material gains. Discovering your calling requires introspection, self-awareness, and a willingness to explore different paths. It may not be immediately apparent or easily defined, but it resides within the deepest corners of your being. It involves understanding your unique strengths, passions, and values and aligning them with the needs of the world around you.

When you pursue your calling, you tap into a wellspring of motivation that propels you forward, even in the face of adversity. When you find yourself energized by your work, it feels like time is flying, and it seems effortless. A calling can lead to a profound sense of fulfillment, bringing harmony and balance to your life as you strive to live out your purpose.

Key Nugget

Key Nugget for Chapter Nine: Resistance and fear sometimes accompany transformation, even when embracing your calling. Recognize that as you grow in pursuing your passions and dreams, there should be growth in that pursuit. Pay attention to the way this growth is affecting you, so you can remain proactive about not being overwhelmed. Your calling has a profound impact on others, but you must remember how it impacts you in the process as well.

Chapter 9 Questions to Ponder

What factors should be taken into consideration when selecting your chosen career path?

How can your career reflect your values and sense of purpose?

Can you distinguish the difference between your career and your calling?

Thoughts:

Chapter 10 – It May Be Time to Pivot

Teaching can be an immensely satisfying profession with unique challenges, but at some point, you may feel it necessary to move on and explore other opportunities. In this chapter, we look at five indicators that suggest it's time to leave their careers behind.

Mr. Jones' Need for Transition

After ten years of enjoying teaching high school math, Mr. Jones felt unfulfilled. Every day, he found himself counting down the hours until his class ended, struggling to stay motivated in the workplace. It became clear – it was time for a change. Mr. Jones decided to make this change by transitioning into Educational Administration, leaving behind students and colleagues he loved deeply. But deep down inside, he knew this decision was essential to his personal and professional development.

Five Signs Suggesting It's Time to Pivot or Leave

> *"We must remember this truth: you cannot pour from an empty cup." - Unknown*

The idea of leaving or moving on feels scary to some because they assume it is the same as giving up. We must be aware of the signals that warn us not to "give up," but it is time to move on for the good of ourselves and others. Here are some signs to look out for.

1. **Burnout and Lack of Passion.** If teaching has become too taxing for you to enjoy, and no new ideas or opportunities arise from your work, now may be a good time for a change.

2. **No Growth and Development.** If professional growth seems to leave you stuck, and you no longer feel inspired in your current role, now may be the right time to explore alternative paths.

3. **Consistently Poor Work-Life Balance.** If teaching has become all-consuming for you, and you struggle to keep this from happening, it's time to find another job with a more favorable work-life balance.

4. **Misalignment with Your Values and Mission Statement.** If the school or district's values don't align with your own (or your values conflict with other members of your team), it may be worth it to explore alternative opportunities.

5. **Compromises to Your Health or Well-Being.** If your work environment is adversely affecting your emotional and psychological well-being, it may be worthwhile to explore other options. If your workplace has become toxic for any reason, now may be the right time to make adjustments and change.

Making the difficult but essential decision to leave can be challenging but necessary for personal and professional growth. Recognizing indicators like the ones listed above can assist in making informed decisions and continually impacting lives in a positive way. Put yourself first, so you can continue making an impactful difference for all involved.

Typical Reasons Teachers Change Careers

1. **Burnout.** Teaching can be emotionally and physically draining work. It becomes all too easy for teachers to experience burnout due to heavy workloads, long hours, ill support from administrators, and high-stressed environments. Teachers experiencing burnout typically feel physically, emotionally, and mentally exhausted, which can result in their search for alternative professions with lower stress levels and a better work-life balance.

2. **Low Pay:** Teaching can be financially taxing, which could cause some educators to leave education altogether in search of higher-paying positions. This is especially true if you have student loan debt or other obligations to meet. Teachers may have reached a professional plateau in education, prompting them to seek opportunities outside this sector for further growth and development. Without clear growth prospects available, teachers may feel that their growth prospects have reached a dead end and seek alternative routes that offer greater potential for advancement.

Conclusion

Burnout and low pay are the top two drivers pushing teachers away from the profession, but there is one rebuttal that compels many to stay – their connection with the students. Teachers often form strong bonds with their students, making it hard to leave entirely. Feelings of responsibility could prevent this decision from escaping because leaving feels like abandonment to both the educator and students. It's important for teachers to examine the full picture when deciding to leave or stay.

Key Nugget

Key Nugget for Chapter Ten: It takes courage and resilience to embrace the journey of pivoting in a new direction that aligns with your evolving passions and aspirations. The feeling of being stuck, lacking fulfillment, or desire for a deeper calling are common indications that your current path may no longer serve you. Take the time to assess your transferable skills, research new opportunities, and develop a plan, so you can gain a sense of direction and alleviate the drain of uncertainty.

Chapter 10 Questions to Ponder

What are some warning signs that it might be time for a change?

How can you differentiate temporary difficulties from more pressing concerns which require action?

What steps can you take to prepare should a career transition become necessary?

Thoughts:

Chapter 11 – I Need A Boost

Now that we've reviewed all the components of remaining "energized" (while also considering the need to transition careers), it's time to summarize these components into a plan. We must fully engage in the "I Need a Boost" Strategy.

1. **Cultivating Relationships.** This is the initial step in the "I Need A Boost" strategy. Teachers should connect with people who can assist them in reaching their goals, including colleagues, administrators, students, and community partners. Building these connections requires dedication and honesty. When educators connect with others, they create an invaluable network and support to help them overcome difficulties and succeed in their careers.

2. **Becoming the Person You Want to Be.** For this second step, educators should assess their strengths and weaknesses, set goals and devise plans to reach them. This also involves the need to align values with the vision of success; and align values with the concept of success to become who you want to be to find more fulfillment, engagement, and effectiveness in your roles.

3. **Balance School and Life.** Educators should set priorities and boundaries to avoid burnout. The best way to do this is by creating a schedule that includes work, family time, hobbies, and self-care. By managing both aspects of their lives properly, they can avoid burnout while achieving success both in and out of the classroom.

4. **Making the Impossible Into Reality.** In this fourth step, you must review what *appears* impossible, recognize the possibilities, and make them a reality. Educators should adopt a growth mindset, set ambitious goals, and pursue them despite obstacles or setbacks. By believing in what seems impossible and making it happen, educators can inspire their students while simultaneously creating an atmosphere of achievement and resilience within the school environment.

5. **Proactive Steps to Breaking Barriers.** The fifth step consists of you proactively taking steps to recognize and

address any barriers preventing them from reaching their goals; seeking support and resources when needed; taking risks when necessary; and learning from past failures and future successes. When they successfully break through barriers, they can unlock their full potential while making an impactful difference to their students and community members.

The Five B's of Success

Overall, the "I Need a Boost" strategy entails the Five B's of Success:

1. **Building** relationships

2. **Becoming** the person you want to be

3. **Balancing** school life with personal life

4. **Believing** in what appears impossible but making it possible

5. **Breaking** through barriers.

By following these steps, educators can overcome burnout, achieve their goals, and enjoy a meaningful educational career.

Kacey's Story of Success

At one point in graduate school, Kacey found herself feeling stressed out by trying to balance coursework, research, and personal life responsibilities. At times, she doubted her ability to succeed until she came across the "How to Eat an Elephant" strategy, which helped break her goals into manageable pieces.

At first, she focused on forming relationships with peers and professors. To do so, she joined a research group, connecting with like-minded students with similar goals and interests. Together, they supported each other with projects while offering feedback and encouragement.

As Kacey explored becoming the person she desired to be, she identified her strengths in research and writing while realizing she needed to hone her presentation and networking abilities. With that goal in mind, she set a goal of attending more conferences and workshops to gain practical experience and sharpen her skills. Additionally, she worked on improving her mindset by remembering the positive aspects of her work and reminding herself of past accomplishments.

After graduating, her focus shifted towards finding balance in her school and personal life. To this end, she ensured that she scheduled time for self-care activities (such as exercise and hobbies), set boundaries around work hours, and learned to say no to additional commitments that might over-extend her.

At last, she took what seemed impossible and made it possible. She applied for a competitive fellowship that she seemed unlikely to receive, yet was honored when selected. This provided an incredible opportunity for her to pursue her research goals and gain invaluable experience.

"When burnout threatens to consume you, a boost is the lifeline that empowers you to reclaim your joy, redefine your boundaries, and nourish your sight." -Unknown

The "I Need a Boost" strategy helped Kacey overcome burnout and succeed. It taught her that – by breaking her goals into manageable steps, building relationships, enhancing strengths, and maintaining balance – she could unlock her full potential and reach it.

Conclusion

As we draw nearer to the end of this book, it becomes clear that being an educator can be both challenging and exhausting. Yet, through employing the five B's, we can surmount obstacles to personal and professional growth and overcome any hurdles along the way. By building strong relationships with students and colleagues, becoming lifelong learners, balancing work life with personal life, believing in ourselves and our abilities, and breaking down barriers that impede success, educators can survive and thrive as educators. These strategies can give us the boost we need to push through when we feel like giving up. Remember, success may never come quickly, but perseverance and determination can achieve great things in our careers while leaving a positive mark on students' lives.

# Key Nugget

Key Nugget for Chapter Eleven: The demands of standardized testing, administrative requirements, and societal expectations can take a toll on your well-being and diminish your motivation. By aligning your drive with your values and original purpose, you can regain a sense of control and reignite your passion for education. By recognizing how what's driving you could be draining you and implementing strategies for self-care, growth, and balance, you can reclaim your energy and find renewed inspiration.

Chapter 11 Questions to Ponder

How can you recognize when motivation or energy needs to be restored?

Which strategies have proven most successful at improving mood and productivity?

What or who is draining your energy and motivation?

Thoughts:

Chapter 12 – The Power of Your Presence

No matter your profession, knowing whether your work makes a meaningful contribution to society can be daunting. Sometimes we may feel like just another cog in an intricate machine and question our relevance. I want you to know that every presence matters greatly and is vitally necessary. Educators, counselors, nurses, teachers, administrators, or factory workers all count immensely! I want you to remember you are essential, and the impact of your presence cannot be understated!

> *"Someone's destiny is tied to your assignment"* -Mansfield Key III

Think about how your presence influences those around you by considering these examples: students may look up to teachers as their only positive role models; patients could rely on nurses for empathy and motivation; colleagues depend on each other for motivational purposes. Indeed, individual presence can uphold and inspire those around us in ways we may never fully comprehend.

Your work affects more than those directly involved with you: its ripples vibrate far and wide. Students you teach could become doctors, scientists, or entrepreneurs who transform society. In the same way, patients that nurses care for could live longer and healthier lives thanks to the care they receive. And colleagues could create products, services, and innovations which have an indirect positive effect on countless others outside of their work environment.

At its core, your presence and work matter. So, if you ever feel powerless to make an impactful difference, remember that even though immediate results may not always be noticeable, your efforts make an impressive statement about who you are! Bill Gates, Martin Luther King Jr., Steve Jobs, Elon Musk, President Barack Obama, and Michael Jordon all have one thing in common; they all had a teacher.

Your presence has far-reaching ramifications for those you assist and those around you. Colleagues, students, patients, and others rely on each other for support, guidance, and encouragement. They also give the same to the people they serve and interact with! Thinking about this encourages me during difficult times; it helps me see value in my work when things look hopeless.

If you need assistance, feel free to reach out for support from colleagues, friends, family, or mentors. When feeling better again, please do your part by supporting and inspiring others to remind them how invaluable their efforts are. If you resist allowing your presence to bring something new or valuable to the table, its absence won't have any lasting ramifications.

Your job assignment has a formative influence on the destiny of others, and they rely on you for knowledge, expertise, passion, and presence. Even when things seem brutal, or you want to give up altogether, remember: each day counts, and you are making a meaningful, impactful contribution that helps shape our world for good!

I am a living example of how teachers' presence and influence can transform lives. I should have been diagnosed with dyslexia as a child; instead, I struggled to read, often felt defeated, and felt isolated until eventually being accepted by my classmates and society as one of their own.

Mrs. Stockard, one of my teachers, soon noticed I was struggling and decided to help. Working directly with me one-on-

one, she taught me how to read while encouraging me along the way. With Mrs. Stockard's assistance, I learned how to read while also expanding my confidence and reading knowledge.

Mrs. Stockard made an immeasurable mark on me; her influence extended well beyond teaching me reading skills. It inspired me to assist other readers who struggled, using similar methods I learned from Mrs. Stockard herself to assist students in learning to read. My natural talent for teaching students increased, as did my passion for helping others achieve reading success.

Throughout my career, I have become an internationally acclaimed speaker who has assisted millions. Our innovative programs utilize technology to make reading accessible and enjoyable for students of all ages. My books, talks at conferences, and media coverage all promote the message of inclusivity. Anyone can learn regardless of their background or ability.

My story is a remarkable testament to teachers' influence on their students.

Through Mrs. Stockard's influence and presence, I was given the tools and support necessary for success. Due to this assistance, I have had the opportunity to inspire millions around the world, encouraging them to never give up their dreams, never give in and keep pushing forward toward making an impactful difference in this world.

Mrs. Stockard introduced me to a beautiful young lady named Sharlene in middle school class. She became my consummate ally. Today we're married with two daughters, and they are also changing lives daily by sharing their journey!

Conclusion

As we wrap up this book, I leave you with several key takeaways. My message in "I Need a Boost" underscores the significance of finding our passion, creating solid relationships, prioritizing self-care, and being flexible when adapting to change. For teachers especially, remaining true to our purpose and committed to our student's success through difficult times remains of utmost importance.

Miss Stockard's story in this book demonstrates the positive effect teachers can have on the lives of their students. Teachers serve not just as instructors but as mentors, role models, and guides who have the power to change lives for good. Let us remember these lessons and stories which have inspired us. By taking control of our lives and drawing upon our strengths, we can reignite the passion, find strength within, and make a positive difference for those we teach together – inspiring, motivating, and empowering them toward reaching their true potential!

Thank you for reading "I Need a Boost!" Let's work together towards building brighter futures for our students.

☛Key Nugget

Key Nugget for Chapter Twelve: Wherever you are in life, it's important to evaluate your contribution. At work, in your home, at church, amongst your friends and family – are you taking up space or making a difference? Are people being impacted by the differences you are making? The answer to this last question is probably yes, so take the question further: is this impact positive or negative? The key to making sure your impact is positive starts with a boost: when you are fully boosted, you can boost others.

Chapter 12 Questions to Ponder

Which nonverbal cues or behaviors contribute to a strong presence?

How can your presence inspire and motivate others?

Thoughts:

> *"If your presence doesn't add value, your absence won't make a difference"* -Unknown

Epilogue

In "I Need a Boost," I realized that our search for validation and motivation is something everyone goes through. We all crave that rush of happiness and satisfaction like dopamine when we achieve our goals or receive praise. But there's a hidden danger that drains our energy and leaves us exhausted.

My goal in writing this book was to give you practical tools to prevent burnout and compassion fatigue while also showing you that you're not alone in this struggle. We all face the challenge of finding fulfillment and recognition.

But here's the surprise: while sharing these strategies, I discovered that helping others and guiding them through these challenges also renewed my energy. Seeking validation is natural, but supporting others can be just as fulfilling.

As you embark on your journey of balance and rejuvenation, remember that it's an ongoing process. Pay attention to signs of exhaustion and embrace practices that nourish your spirit. Take time for stillness, connect with loved ones, do things that bring you joy, and allow yourself to rest.

Together, as we navigate life's ups and downs, let this book remind us of our interconnectedness and shared experiences. Let's show compassion and understanding to one another, creating a supportive network that helps us overcome draining forces.

Life can drain you and zap your energy, but I discovered a few simple remedies. Whether it was my favorite song, a beloved movie, a funny sitcom, or a comforting meal, these small things can give you temporary fulfillment and renewed energy. I'm not recommending these as permanent solutions, but comfort in moments of discomfort and distress can provide a boost to help you endure temporary issues you may face. Hanging with family and friends can bring support and comfort in times of need as well.

May "I Need a Boost" inspire change, encourage balance, and prove the resilience of the human spirit. Cheers to refueling, replenishing, and rediscovering the joy of the journey.

A Personal Note

As we conclude our journey in "I Need a Boost," I must not overlook the one crucial factor that has kept me grounded amidst the chaos of this world. While I've shared numerous tools, tips, and techniques to combat burnout and compassion fatigue, it would be remiss of me not to mention the game-changer that has been my unwavering source of strength: my faith in God. As my favorite scripture, Galatians 6:9 reminds me, "And let us not be weary in well doing: for in due season, we shall reap if we faint not." I firmly believe that my energy and motivation cannot be sustained without God as my ultimate source of strength. Recognizing the presence of a higher power, a divine helper, an eye in the sky, the man upstairs—whatever you may call it—I refer to him as my personal Lord and Savior, the wellspring of my strength and ability. Through daily prayer for guidance, power, and instruction, I have found comfort in God. He has helped me navigate the good and bad days, sustaining my mental, emotional, and spiritual well-being and driving me forward with a higher purpose, even in moments of depletion. As you close this book, may you also discover the incredible power of faith as a driving force in your life, providing the ultimate boost when you need it most. My belief is when you receive help from your faith and assistance from others and couple that with these practical tools, when you feel drained, you are positioning yourself for the ultimate Boost.

Biography

Mansfield Key III is an International Motivational Speaker and leading Growth Development Strategist known to most as Ole Pete Key. He is a coach, consultant, speechwriter, certified HIV/AIDS Instructor, Social Entrepreneur, and mentor.

He has provided technical assistance to the Federal Government's Health and Human Services for all 50 states. He has worked directly with the United States CDC (Centers for Disease Control). Pete has also completed consultant work for the Departments of Education and the Department of Public Health in several states. He has also provided presentations for the Juvenile Justice System, Foster Care System, the Dream Development Center in Johannesburg, South Africa, and Liverpool, England's Hope Organization.

Pete is the founder and creator of the Lunch with The Keys Program. It teaches Character Education to students in grades kindergarten through twelfth. The Lunch with The Keys Program won the Alabama CLAS School of Distinction Award for outstanding services rendered to youth. He also won the Fatherhood Program of the Year and the Humanitarian of the Year award. He has impacted the lives of millions of people through presentations, programs, and products.

He has authored three books and released multiple DVDs,

CDs, and curriculums. His proudest accomplishment, other than his relationship with God, is his devotion to his loving wife, Sharlene, and his two beautiful daughters, Erin Ruth, and Joi Da'Nae. He is a member of the 2016-2017 Leadership Alabama class and the past Rotary president for the Florence Rotary Club. Pete's purpose and passion are sharing his story and strategies to help others. He believes that everyone has something special, but sometimes people need others to help them discover it. Pete believes that the only reason he's still alive is because his assignment to help others is greater than his sin of potentially hurting others, and this is all because of God's grace.

Additional Books and Resources by Mansfield Key III

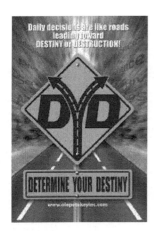

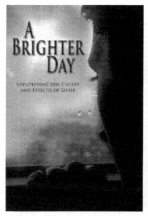

www.Ineedaboostnow.com

Made in the USA
Columbia, SC
21 July 2023

20678790R00072